D1690284

NFL TEAM STORIES

THE STORY OF THE
NEW ENGLAND PATRIOTS

By Jim Gigliotti

Kaleidoscope
Minneapolis, MN

BIGFOOT BOOKS

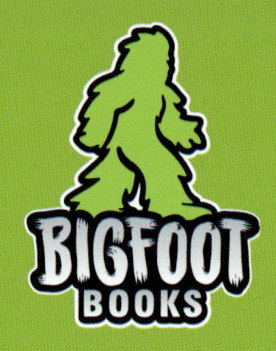

The Quest for Discovery Never Ends

....

This edition first published in 2021 by Kaleidoscope Publishing, Inc.

No part of this publication may be reproduced in whole or in part without written permission of the publisher.

For information regarding permission, write to Kaleidoscope Publishing, Inc.
6012 Blue Circle Drive
Minnetonka, MN 55343

Library of Congress Control Number
2020935947

ISBN
978-1-64519-238-1 (library bound)
978-1-64519-306-7 (ebook)

Text copyright © 2021 by Kaleidoscope Publishing, Inc. All-Star Sports, Bigfoot Books, and associated logos are trademarks and/or registered trademarks of Kaleidoscope Publishing, Inc.

Printed in the United States of America.

FIND ME IF YOU CAN!

Bigfoot lurks within one of the images in this book. It's up to you to find him!

TABLE OF
CONTENTS

Kickoff! 4

Chapter 1: Patriots History 6

Chapter 2: Patriots All-Time Greats 16

Chapter 3: Patriots Superstars 22

Beyond the Book 28
Research Ninja 29
Further Resources 30
Glossary 31
Index 32
Photo Credits 32
About the Author 32

KICKOFF!

Dynasty!

"Dynasty" is a word used in sports a lot. It describes a team that is very good over a long period of time. The Patriots built one of the great dynasties

Here come the Patriots!

in sports. They have been really good for a really long time! The Patriots have not always been a dynasty. They struggled for many years.

The dynasty started with a Super Bowl win in 2001. The team has not let up since. The Patriots have won the Super Bowl six times in all. They are tied for the most Super Bowl wins ever. Let's find out how they became champions!

Chapter 1
Patriots History

The Patriots began play in 1960. They started in the American Football League (AFL). They were called the Boston Patriots. All of the AFL teams joined the NFL in 1970. The Patriots had several home fields until then. One of them was Fenway Park. That is the famous home of baseball's Red Sox.

The Patriots moved to Foxboro in 1971. That is a town close to Boston. The team changed its name to the New England Patriots. The Patriots finally got their own stadium that year. Today, Gillette Stadium is packed every Sunday with Patriots fans.

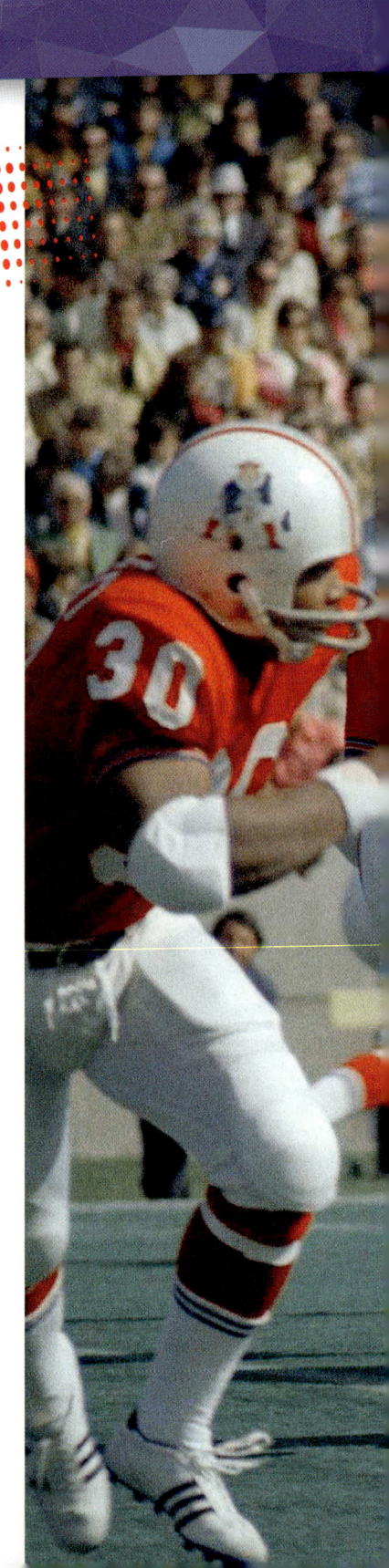

FUN FACT

The Patriots made Jim Plunkett the first pick in the 1971 NFL Draft.

Jim Plunkett

The Patriots had pretty good teams in the late 1970s. Those teams had some of the NFL's best rushing attacks ever. The Patriots won their first AFC title in 1985. They won the AFC East for the first time in 1986.

The team hired Bill "Tuna" Parcells as coach in 1993. Parcells won the Super Bowl twice with the

The Bears clobbered the Patriots in Super Bowl XX.

Drew Bledsoe was sacked often in Super Bowl XXXI.

Giants. He did not lead the Patriots to a Super Bowl win. They came close, though. The Patriots won the AFC in 1996. They lost the Super Bowl to the Packers.

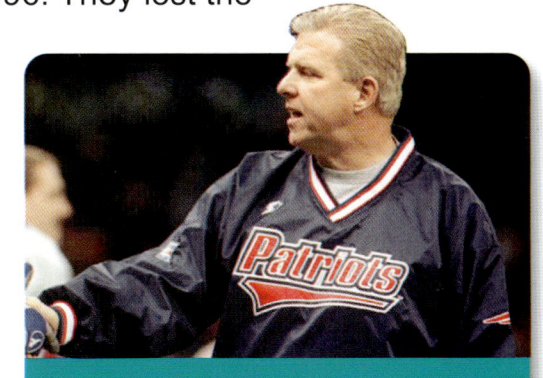

Why Tuna? Parcells said it the first time. He was trying to encourage a player and somehow called himself Charlie Tuna!

The Patriots hired Bill Belichick as coach in 2000. They **drafted** quarterback Tom Brady the same year. Both moves sure turned out well! The two men helped the Patriots win the Super Bowl three times in four years beginning in 2001. The team had a record-setting year in 2007. The Patriots won all 16 **regular-season** games. No team had ever done that! They lost the Super Bowl to the Giants, though.

FUN FACT

The Miami Dolphins went 14–0 in 1971. That was the record until the Patriots broke it in 2007.

Bill Belichick

The Patriots won the Super Bowl again in 2014. Their fifth Super Bowl win came in 2016. It was their most amazing victory. They trailed the Falcons 28–3 in the third quarter. They were still down 16 points late in the fourth period. The Pats scored two touchdowns. They made two **two-point conversions**. The game went to **overtime**. The Patriots scored. They won 34–28. What a comeback!

The Patriots lost the Super Bowl in 2017. They won their sixth title in 2018. They beat the Los Angeles Rams 13–3.

The 2019 season ended with a loss in the playoffs. It was still another great season. The Patriots won 12 games. They finished in first place in the AFC East. This dynasty shows no signs of slowing down!

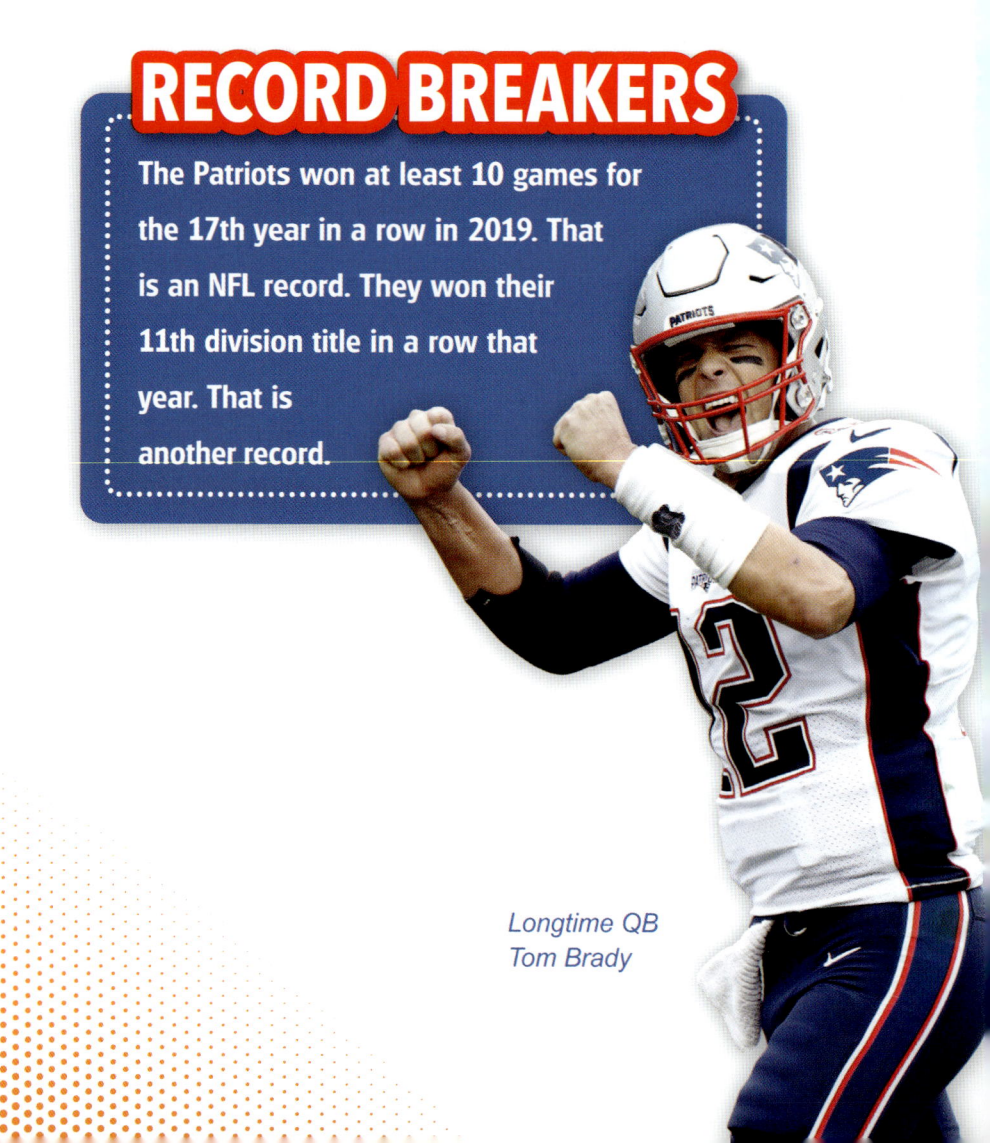

RECORD BREAKERS

The Patriots won at least 10 games for the 17th year in a row in 2019. That is an NFL record. They won their 11th division title in a row that year. That is another record.

Longtime QB Tom Brady

TIMELINE OF THE NEW ENGLAND PATRIOTS

1960
1960: The Patriots begin play in the AFL.

1970
1970: The Patriots join the NFL.

1985
1985: The team wins its first AFC title.

2001
2001: The Patriots win the first of a record-tying six Super Bowls.

2009
2009: The Patriots win the first of a record 11 division titles in a row.

2016
2016: The team wins with the greatest comeback in Super Bowl history.

2019
2019: The Patriots win 10-plus games for the 17th year in a row.

THE START OF IT ALL

Few people expected the Patriots to be good in 2001. Then their starting quarterback got hurt early in the season. Even fewer people expected them to be good! But Tom Brady stepped in.

Brady led the Patriots to the playoffs. That was a surprise. They went on to the Super Bowl. That was a surprise, too. Then they won it all. That was the biggest surprise. The Rams were big favorites to win the Super Bowl. The score was tied late in the game. Brady marched his team to a field-goal try. Adam Vinatieri stepped up. He kicked the ball. The Patriots and all the fans watched and waited. The kick was good! The Patriots won 20–17.

FUN FACT

Two years after kicking this game-winning field goal, Viniatieri did it again in Super Bowl XXXVIII!

Chapter 2
Patriots All-Time Greats

Many experts call Tom Brady the "GOAT." That stands for Greatest of All Time. Brady passes for a lot of yards. He throws for a lot of touchdowns. He is second on the NFL's all-time lists in those stats. But mostly he wins. He has more wins than any QB ever. He has the most Super Bowl wins, too.

Brady made the Pro Bowl 14 times in 20 seasons with the Patriots. He became a free agent for the first time in 2020. That meant he was free to sign with any team. He chose to sign with Tampa Bay. Patriots fans were very sad!

Tom Brady was a great leader for the Pats.

Wes Welker was Brady's top receiver. He set a team record for catches. He played six seasons beginning in 2007. He caught more than 100 passes in five of those years. Tight end Rob Gronkowski was a key receiver near the goal line. "Gronk" scored more touchdowns than anyone else in Pats history. Kevin Faulk was a running back who did it all. He ran the ball. He caught passes. He returned kicks. Tom Brady helped make these players better. And they helped make Brady better!

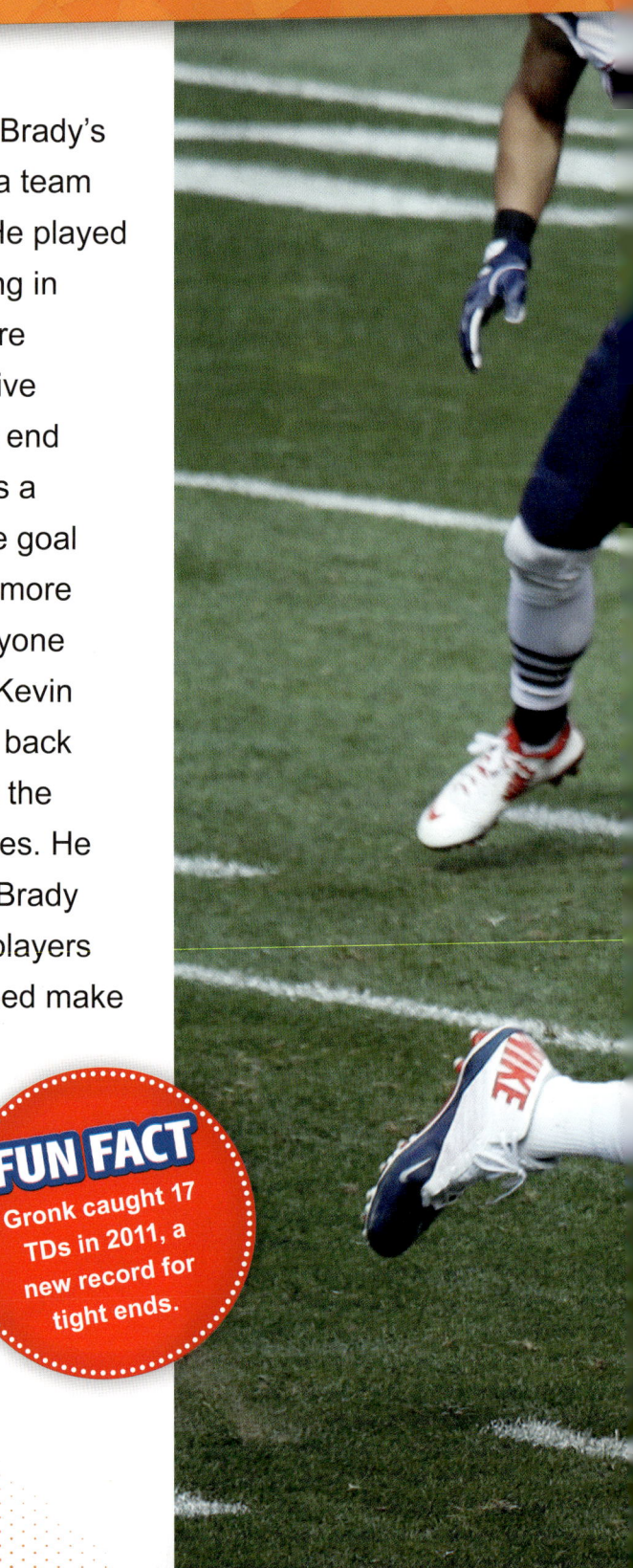

FUN FACT

Gronk caught 17 TDs in 2011, a new record for tight ends.

Rob Gronkowski

The Patriots had great players before their dynasty began. Guard John Hannah was a star blocker in the 1970s and '80s. He was the first Patriots player to make the Hall of Fame. Sam Cunningham ran for the most yards in team history. Stanley Morgan had the most receiving yards.

Linebacker Andre Tippett had the most sacks in team history. He is in the Hall of Fame. So is star cornerback Mike Haynes.

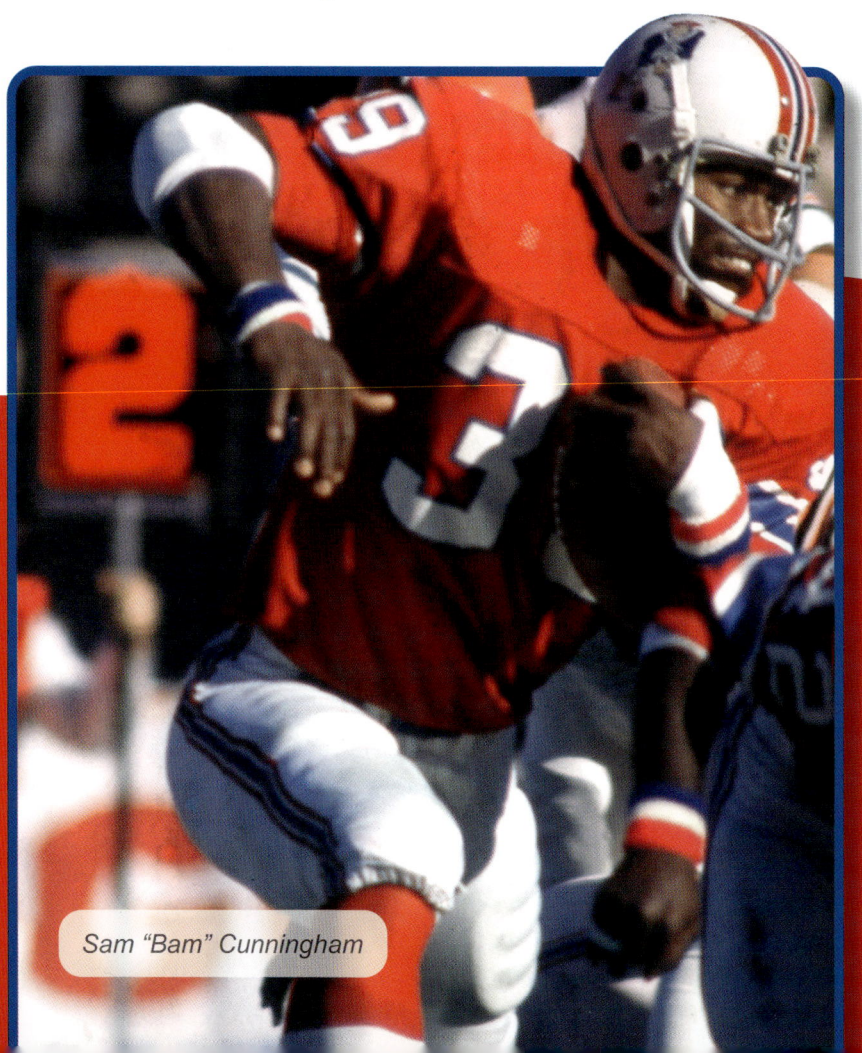

Sam "Bam" Cunningham

PATRIOTS RECORDS

These players piled up the best stats in Patriots history. The numbers are career records through the 2019 season.

Total TDs: Rob Gronkowski, 80

TD Passes: Tom Brady, 541

Passing Yards: Tom Brady, 74,571

Rushing Yards: Sam Cunningham, 5,453

Receptions: Wes Welker, 672

Points: Stephen Gostkowski, 1,775

Sacks: Andre Tippett, 100

Chapter 3
Patriots Superstars

The offense usually makes the headlines for the Patriots. In 2019, it was the defense's turn. It was No. 1 in the NFL. The Patriots allowed the fewest yards and points in the league. That defense included one of the league's top players. Cornerback Stephon Gilmore tied for the NFL lead with six **interceptions**. Two of them were "pick sixes." That means he returned them for touchdowns! Gilmore led the NFL with 20 passes **defensed**. He was a first-team all-pro pick.

FUN FACT

Gilmore was named the 2019 NFL Defensive Player of the Year.

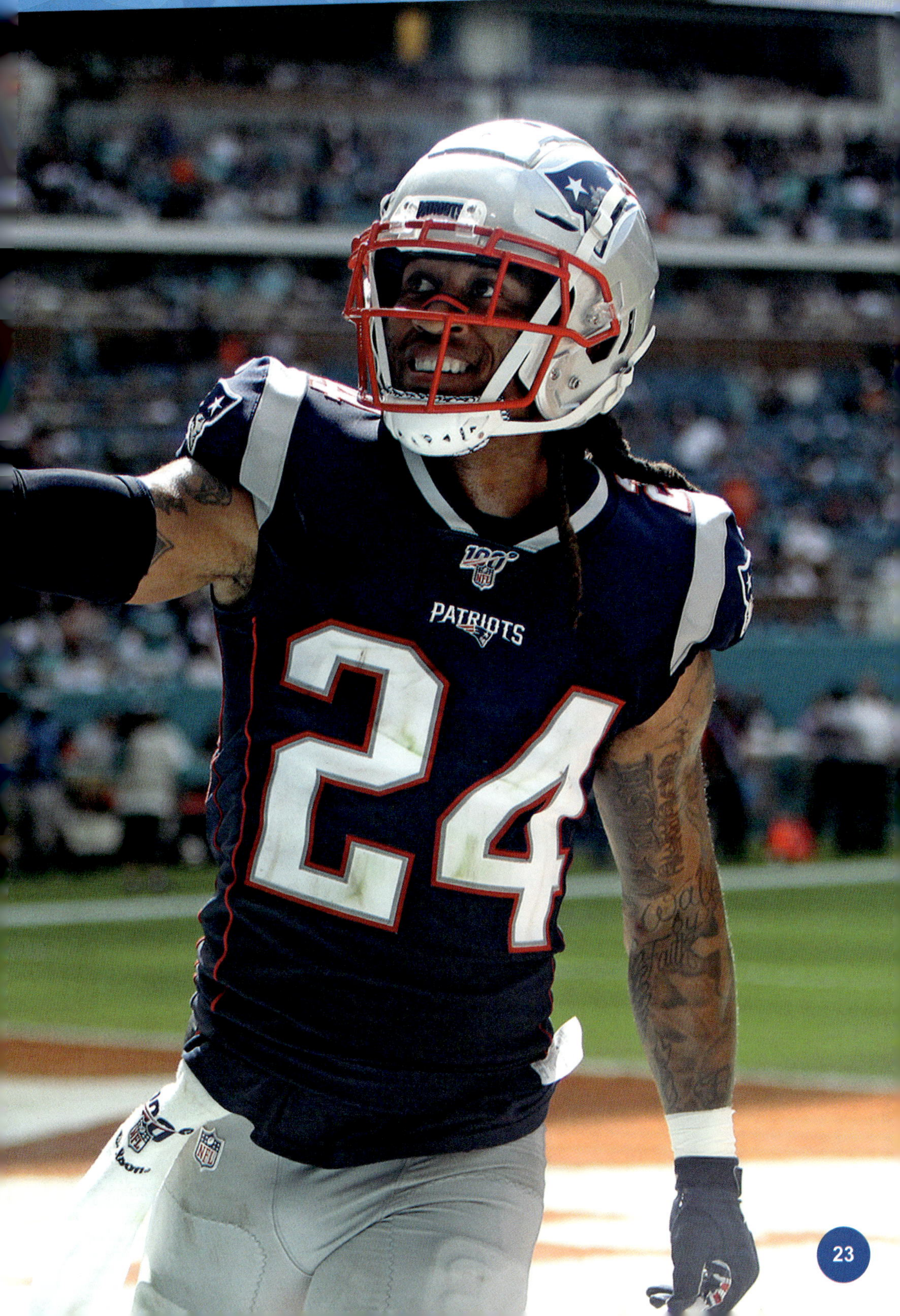
PATRIOTS
24

Linebacker Dont'a Hightower is another great Patriots defender. He is a **team captain**. He made the Pro Bowl in 2019 for the second time.

Running back James White is another team captain. He is a great pass catcher out of the backfield. The Patriots drafted running back Sony Michel in 2018. He has sparked the team's ground game. Julian Edelman is the team's top receiver. He has more than 1,000 yards in each of three seasons. He caught exactly 100 passes in 2019.

James White

Julian Edelman

Matthew Slater

The Patriots are always good on **special teams**.

Matthew Slater has a very important role. Slater covers kickoffs and punts. He is very good at it. He helps the Patriots keep good field position. Slater made the Pro Bowl for the eighth time in 2019.

The 2020 season was different for the Patriots. It was their first without Brady since 1999. Belichick is still around, though. He seems to able to win with anyone.

In all areas, the Patriots are still among the best. They need those great players to keep the dynasty going!

BEYOND
THE BOOK

After reading the book, it's time to think about what you learned. Try the following exercises to jumpstart your ideas.

RESEARCH

FIND OUT MORE. Where would you go to find out more about your favorite NFL teams and players? Check out NFL.com, of course. Each team also has its own website. What other sports information sites can you find? See if you can find other cool facts about your favorite team.

CREATE

GET ARTISTIC. Each NFL team has a logo. The Patriots logo includes a man wearing a Revolutionary-War era hat. Get some art materials and try designing your own Patriots logo. Or create a new team and make a logo for it. What colors would you choose? How would you draw the mascot?

DISCOVER

GO DEEP! This book writes that the Patriots were an NFL dynasty. Find out if there were other dynasties in NFL history. What about other sports? Were there dynasties in Major League Baseball, the NBA, or the NHL? Which do think was the top dynasty in all of sports?

GROW

GET OUT AND PLAY! You don't need to be in the NFL to enjoy football. You just need a football and some friends. Play touch or tag football. Or you can hang cloth flags from your belt; grab the belt and make the "tackle." See who has the best arm to be quarterback. Who is the best receiver? Who can run the fastest? Time to play football!

RESEARCH NINJA

Visit www.ninjaresearcher.com/2381 to learn how to take your research skills and book report writing to the next level!

RESEARCH

DIGITAL LITERACY TOOLS

SEARCH LIKE A PRO
Learn about how to use search engines to find useful websites.

FACT OR FAKE?
Discover how you can tell a trusted website from an untrustworthy resource.

TEXT DETECTIVE
Explore how to zero in on the information you need most.

SHOW YOUR WORK
Research responsibly— learn how to cite sources.

WRITE

GET TO THE POINT
Learn how to express your main ideas.

PLAN OF ATTACK
Learn prewriting exercises and create an outline.

DOWNLOADABLE REPORT FORMS

Further Resources

BOOKS

Christopher, Matt. *On the Field With . . . Tom Brady*. New York: Hachette Book Group, 2018.

Cooper, Robert. *New England Patriots (Inside the NFL)*. Mendota Heights, Minn: North Star Editions, 2019.

Levit, Joe. *Football's G.O.A.T.* Minneapolis: Lerner Publishing Group, 2020.

WEBSITES

FACTSURFER

Factsurfer.com gives you a safe, fun way to find more information.

1. Go to www.factsurfer.com.
2. Enter "New England Patriots" into the search box and click.
3. Select your book cover to see a list of related websites.

Glossary

defensed: stopped from catching. Gilmore defensed the pass by knocking it down.

drafted: chosen in the NFL's selection of college players. In 2000, the Patriots drafted Tom Brady with the 199th overall selection.

dynasty: a group that is successful over a long period. With six Super Bowl wins, the Patriots are an NFL dynasty.

interceptions: passes caught by the defense. The Patriots stopped the Miami QB with three interceptions.

overtime: extra time added when a 60-minute game ends in a tie. The Patriots tied the game at 28–28. They won in overtime 31–28.

regular season: the 16 games on the NFL's schedule before the playoffs. The Patriots' regular-season record was 10–6.

special teams: football units that are not offense or defense. Punters and kickers are key parts of special teams.

team captain: a player chosen to represent his teammates as a leader. Slater is the special teams captain for New England.

two-point conversion: after a TD is scored, a team can attempt this from the two-yard line. Brady hit Gronk with a pass to score the two-point conversion.

Index

American Football League (AFL), 6
Atlanta Falcons, 11
Belichick, Bill, 10, 27
Boston Patriots, 6
Boston Red Sox, 6
Brady, Tom, 10, 14, 16, 18, 27
Cunningham, Sam, 20
Edelman, Julian, 24
Faulk, Kevin, 18
Fenway Park, 6
Foxboro, 6
Gillette Stadium, 6
Gilmore, Stephon, 22
Gronkowski, Rob, 18
Hannah, John, 20
Haynes, Mike, 20
Hightower, Dont'a, 24
Los Angeles Rams, 12, 14
Michel, Sony, 24
New York Giants, 9, 10
Parcells, Bill "Tuna," 8, 9
Slater, Matthew, 27
Super Bowl, 5, 8, 9, 10, 11, 12, 14, 16
Tampa Bay Buccaneers, 16
Tippett, Andre, 20
Vinatieri, Adam, 14
Welker, Wes, 18
White, James, 24

PHOTO CREDITS

The images in this book are reproduced through the courtesy of: AP Images: AP Images: Charles Krupa 4; Walter Green 6; Lennox McLendon 8; Dave Martin 9; Glenn Osmundson/KRT 9 inset; NFL Photos 14; Tony Tomsic 20. Focus on Football: 12, 16, 19, 24, 25. Newscom: John Kuntz 10; Rich Graessle/Icon SW 11; Lionel Hahn/MCT 18; David Santiago/TNS 22; Matthew Healy/UPI 26. **Cover photo:** Focus on Football.

About the Author

Jim Gigliotti was an editor at NFL Publishing for many years. Now he writes books for young readers.